Project Management Instit

D1284575

Challenges and Best Practices of Managing Government Projects and Programs

Young Hoon Kwak, PhD
Min Liu, PhD
Peerasit Patanakul, PhD
Ofer Zwikael, PhD, PMP

ISBN: 978-1-62825-065-7

Published by: Project Management Institute, Inc.
                                  14 Campus Boulevard
                                  Newtown Square, Pennsylvania 19073-3299 USA
                                  Phone: +610-356-4600
                                  Fax: +610-356-4647
                                  Email: customercare@pmi.org
                                  Internet: www.PMI.org

PMI Publications welcomes corrections and comments on its books. Please feel free to send comments on typographical, formatting, or other errors. Simply make a copy of the relevant page of the book, mark the error, and send it to: Book Editor, PMI Publications, 14 Campus Boulevard, Newtown Square, PA 19073-3299 USA.

To inquire about discounts for resale or educational purposes, please contact the PMI Book Service Center.

                                  PMI Book Service Center
                                  P.O. Box 932683, Atlanta, GA 31193-2683 USA
                                  Phone: 1-866-276-4764 (within the U.S. or Canada) or
                                  +1-770-280-4129 (globally)
                                  Fax: +1-770-280-4113
                                  Email: info@bookorders.pmi.org

Table of Contents

Executive Summary

Governments fund projects and programs to achieve national growth and implement long-term national objectives. Because of the different goals, objectives, and circumstances that these initiatives unfold, they often suffer from additional challenges and complexities, which in turn cause high failure rates. The goal of this research is to provide a better understanding of the key characteristics of government projects by reviewing audit reports and related public documents and providing a series of recommendations to improve governmental project management practices. This research is particularly timely as large government projects and programs greatly contribute to economic recovery and development.

Particular focus was given to large-scale and complex megaprojects and programs as many of the government-initiated and funded projects fall into this category. A total of 39 government projects and programs in developed countries (18 in the United States, 15 in Australia, and the remaining six in the United Kingdom) were analyzed based on official government audit reports. These projects also represented three different sectors; 13 from the infrastructure and transportation sector, nine from Information Technology/Information System (IT/IS) (Information and Communications Technology in the UK and Australia), eight from the defense sector, and nine involving more than one sector. The average duration of all the projects and programs was 8.8 years, with the average cost of US$13 billion.

Based on the content analysis and evaluation of collected information, it was important to establish an overall framework that fit well with government projects and programs. As a result, six key characteristics of government projects and programs have been identified. These include (1) pursuing non-financial benefits, (2) being susceptible to political environment and dynamics, (3) following a mandated project management process, (4) being a large and complex megaproject, (5) having a long product life cycle, and (6) dealing with multiple stakeholders.

To provide valuable implications for practitioners, this research identifies key lessons learned and suggests key success factors for managing government projects effectively. Recommendations to assist and improve project management performance are presented, discussed, and illustrated based on the following six key characteristics of government projects and programs.

1. Pursuing non-financial benefits

- Identify clear non-financial benefits in the business case;
- Ensure that target benefits are realistic and achievable;
- Establish an agreed-upon evaluation methodology for project benefits; and
- Evaluate the impact of the project on the achievement of strategic goals.

2. Being susceptible to political environment and dynamics

- Consider legal consultation to ensure that proposed ideas are in line with current legislation;
- Consider financial consultation to improve understanding of economic aspects of the project;
- Ensure that the project is aligned with strategies of the agencies;
- Consider public-private partnerships (PPPs) when appropriate;
- Ensure PPPs are economically feasible; and
- Provide project managers more authority.

3. Following a mandated project management process

- Establish and follow government project management framework and processes;
- Follow formal planning and estimating processes that incorporate lessons learned;
- Follow a formal risk management process;
- Follow formal project monitoring and change management processes; and
- Establish and follow a project governance framework.

4. Being a large and complex megaproject

- Develop a base cost estimate and Integrated Master Schedule (IMS) for megaprojects;
- Align project cost with the annual budget cycle;

- Consider using off-the-shelf solutions rather than high-risk new development when possible;
- Split programs into smaller manageable projects for greater project oversight;
- Develop a contingency plan and monitor risks; and
- Identify training needs for long projects.

5. Having a long product life cycle

- Ensure robust design and quality management process; and
- Carefully consider technologies to avoid those that are still unapproved or too advanced, as well as existing technologies that will soon be obsolete.

6. Dealing with multiple stakeholders

- Engage procurement personnel on the project team;
- Consult the business community when relevant;
- Coordinate the project with existing operations;
- Establish interagency agreements for cross-agency projects; and
- Ensure effective collaboration with procurement personnel and an effective acquisition process.

Statistical analysis has also been conducted to provide better understanding of the relationship between project management capabilities and project management success, using four project-type dimensions of government projects and programs. The results of the analysis are as follows:

- Novelty–Project management positively affects performance in low and medium levels of novelty (derivative and platform), but not in breakthrough projects;
- Technology–Project management positively affects performance in low to high levels of technology (low, medium, and high), but not in projects that involve super-high technology;
- Complexity–Project management positively affects performance in very complex projects (array), but not in projects with low and medium levels of complexity (assembly, system); and
- Pace–Project management positively affects performance in time-critical projects, but not in regular, fast, and blitz projects.

The findings of this research could influence policy makers, government officials, project managers, and the general public to rethink the importance of adopting project management principles, tools, and techniques for government projects and programs that would enhance project efficiency and benefit realization. It will also help practitioners make better decisions relative to large-scale, complex government projects. This research contributes to the body of knowledge describing the challenges and opportunities for applying and implementing project management principles in the government sector.

Acknowledgements

The authors would like to thank the Project Management Institute (PMI) for providing research grants to conduct this study. The findings, analysis, and recommendations of this research are solely the views of the authors and do not necessarily reflect those of the governments described, the governments' auditing agencies, or PMI.

Chapter 1

Introduction

1.1 Motivations and Objectives

Successful implementation of government projects and programs requires a great deal of planning, coordination, and collaboration that should be done through established processes, strong team effort, and involvement of multiple stakeholders. Management of government projects and programs is a challenge for government officials and project managers often because a formal process is not in place, project objectives are not clearly identified, and the costs and benefits of the deliverables are difficult to justify and measure. Government projects and programs also tend to have a long duration, a large budget, multiple stakeholders, and a great deal of uncertainties that make them difficult to plan, implement, and manage effectively.

The application and performance of project and program management in government agencies has been historically poor as reported by the U.S. Government Accountability Office (GAO), the UK National Audit Office (NAO), and the Australian National Audit Office (ANAO) and others. Many government projects and programs are prolonged for years, failing to meet the projects' objectives, wasting taxpayers' money, or they are abruptly terminated in the midst of planning or implementation. Due to the fact that primary funding for government projects comes partially or entirely from constituents, government projects and programs are often scrutinized and criticized by the general public, which exacerbates the image of government as a whole.

This research investigated recurring problems and challenges leading to the poor performance of government projects. Specifically, the past performance and management challenges of large government projects in developed countries (United States, United Kingdom, and Australia) were studied to evaluate estimating, planning, management, control, and close-out practices of government projects. The study covered both government-initiated and funded projects from three major sectors: transportation and infrastructure; defense and space; and information systems development and deployment. Particular focus was given to large-scale and complex megaprojects and programs as many of the government-initiated and funded projects fall into this category.

By investigating projects and programs of different countries and across sectors, this research identified challenges and problems associated with managing government projects and programs. Previously, organizations have proposed modified approaches for the management of government projects and programs, including PMI's *Government Extension to the PMBOK® Guide Third Edition*. The key findings of this study will help practitioners make better decisions when they are involved in large-scale, complex government projects. To provide valuable implications to practitioners, this research suggests key lessons learned and identifies key success factors for effectively managing governmental projects.

This research also contributes to the body of knowledge that describes the challenges and opportunities related to applying and implementing project management principles in government. This research is very timely as large government projects and programs greatly contribute to economic recovery and development. Practical implications of this study include the enhancement of decisions made by policy makers, government officials, and project managers in various governments around the world, specifically to better use project management principles, tools, and techniques.

1.2 Literature Review

A comprehensive literature review was conducted on previous research to better understand current project and program management practices in government. The literature review included government reports, whitepapers, and memos to explore research methods, lessons learned, and strategic roadmaps that have been suggested, if any. The literature reviews are divided into three categories to capture issues related to managing government projects and programs: poor performance management; challenges of megaproject management; and efforts to improve project performance.

1.2.1 Poor Performance Management of Government Projects and Programs

Previous studies of government projects from the United States, United Kingdom, Australia, and other nations with the focus on government IT/IS projects, defense department programs, and large transportation projects show poor performance of managing projects in terms of cost, schedule, and deliverables. Generally, the problems related to system management, governance, project management, contract management, and acquisition management are common (Arditi, Akan, & Gurdamar, 1985; Han, Yun, Kim, Kwak, Park, & Lee, 2009; Kwak & Smith, 2009; Patanakul & Omar, 2010).

Patanakul and Omar (2010) found the common reasons for poor performance of government IT/IS projects related to system management, governance, project management, and contract management. Kwak and Smith (2009) explored key aspects involved in managing risk associated with acquisition projects within the U.S. Department of Defense in order to identify the strengths and weaknesses of overall program management practices by reviewing and analyzing various U.S. GAO reports. Han et al. (2009) provided guidelines and lessons learned to better identify critical causes of schedule delays and cost overruns for evaluating mega transportation project performance. Kwak and Anbari (2010, 2012) investigated the full range of technical, financial, managerial, and organizational effects of applying Earned Value Management (EVM) principles. Their findings contributed to knowledge and practice in this area, and greater opportunities for implementation of EVM in government for objective measurement of project performance and progress.

The main causes for delay of government-initiated construction projects include inadequate resources, public agencies' and contractors' financial difficulties, organizational deficiencies and delays in design work, frequent change orders, and considerable extra work (Arditi, Akan, & Gurdamar 1985; Park, J.R., Park, Y.K., & Kim 2005; Gil, 2007). Insufficient risk management also contributes significantly to project delays and cost overruns in managing government projects (Baldry, 1998; Tysseland, 2008; Kwak & Smith, 2009; Patanakul & Omar, 2010). Dvir (2005) found that customer participation in the development process and end-user preparations have the highest impact on project success. A clear understanding of users' requirements, a proper project classification prior to project initiation, and a carefully selected management style may lead to better implementation and to an increased chance of project success (Shenhar & Dvir, 1996; Shenhar & Bonen, 1997; Shenhar, 1998; Dvir, Raz, & Shenhar, 2003).

1.2.2 Challenges of Managing Large and Complex Projects and Programs

Overly optimistic owners and project managers greatly contribute to cost overruns and schedule delays of megaprojects (Lovallo & Kahneman, 2003). In the pursuit of successful project performance, time control is one of the most important functions, especially in megaprojects where various risk variables cause schedule delays (Jolivet & Navarre, 1996). Schedule delays are a source of great distress to both owners and contractors, mainly because time overruns are directly or indirectly connected with cost overruns (Majid & McCaffer, 1998; Frimpong & Oluwoye, 2003; Lyer & Jha, 2006; Han et al., 2009). Consequently, both researchers and practitioners have focused continually on the analysis of schedule delays in megaprojects (Morris & Hough, 1987; Assaf, Al-Khalil, & Al-Hazmi, 1995; Chan & Kumaraswamy, 1995; Yeo, 1995; Flyvbjerg, Bruzelious, & Rothengatter, 2003b; Williams, 2003).

Poor performance in infrastructure and capital megaprojects relative to cost and time most often results in cost overruns (Stannard, 1990; Merrow, McDonnell, & Argüden, 1988; Flyvbjerg, Holm, & Buhl, 2003a; Flyvbjerg et al., 2003b; Flyvbjerg, Holm, & Buhl, 2004; Flyvbjerg, 2007). In addition, the complexity of megaprojects brings challenges to quality control. Complexity of large government projects is constituted of structural complexity, the number and interdependence of elements, and uncertainty in goals and means (Bruelious, Flyvberg, & Rothengatter, 1998; Kwak, Walewski, Sleeper, & Sadatsafavi, 2014; Williams, 1999 and 2004; GAO, 2002, 2004a, 2004b, 2005a, 2005b, 2006, 2007a, 2007b, 2007c, and 2007d).

1.2.3 Efforts to Improve Project Performance

Approaches recommended for improving performance of large-scale projects include: project implementation profile methodology (Pinto & Slevin, 1987); three systems perspectives based on the concepts of large-scale living systems, hard systematic thinking, and soft systemic methodology (Yeo, 1995); continuous approval methods (Bhuiyan & Thomson, 1999); human factors integration method (Strain & Preece, 1999); and quality management procedures of ISO 9000 QMS, U.S. Army Corps of Engineers, and American Public Works Association. From an organizational performance perspective, Huemann, Keegan, and Turner (2007) developed a research model of human resource management practices for project-oriented organizations. PMI (2006) developed the *Government Extension to the PMBOK® Guide Third Edition* specifically for government projects. The extension provides an overview of the key processes for projects undertaken in the public sector. It is critical to select the right project, the right process, and the right teams to deliver a quality product.

1.3 Research Approach and Data Analysis

1.3.1 Research Questions

The following research questions have been formulated to gain a better understanding of the problems leading to the poor performance of managing government projects and programs from a global perspective.

- What are the unique characteristics of government projects and programs?
- What is the current performance status of managing government projects and programs in terms of cost, schedule, and other project related variables?
- What are the common reasons for poor performance in managing government projects?
- How do project personnel address the impacts of external issues (e.g., politics, environment, social awareness), managerial issues (e.g., authority, competency, governance

and oversight, information sharing, and decision making), and technical issues (e.g., system requirements, technology, design maturity, and system integration) on the performance of managing government projects?
- What are the key lessons learned from analyzing different government projects and programs?

1.3.2 Content Analysis

This research explores common reasons for poor project performance by the government, analyzes relationships among the performance of government projects and programs and their characteristics (e.g., budget size, duration, scope, and team composition), reports key lessons learned, and provides recommendations to improve project management performance in government. The key lessons learned are captured and classified into a comprehensive database of worldwide government projects and programs that can be used by both practitioners and academics.

Using data from governmental auditing agencies of the respective countries, we conducted content analysis to identify the problems and challenges in managing government projects. To extract the most information from each report, we performed content coding to create groups of problems and challenges for each project, related to the quality of its scoping and approval processes, as well as the way it was managed.

1.3.3 Project Demographics

The research team gathered in-depth information of 39 government projects and programs from the United States, United Kingdom, and Australia (see Appendix A for the complete list of projects and programs). To do so, public information and audit reports from the U.S. GAO, the UK NAO, and the ANAO were collected. Analyzing and evaluating in-depth project performance information from different countries' audit reports provided an objective approach to determine the current state of government projects. The auditing offices are non-partisan and therefore, the information is deemed reliable, factual, and unbiased.

Eighteen of the projects have been executed in the U.S., 15 in Australia, and the remaining six in the United Kingdom. These 39 projects also represent different sectors: 13 from the infrastructure sector, nine from IT/IS (Information and Communications Technology in the United Kingdom and Australia), eight from the defense sector, and nine involve more than one sector. The average duration was 8.8 years with the average cost of US$13 billion.

The projects were analyzed by using project typology framework's four-dimension diamond model proposed by Shenhar and Dvir (2007). This analysis suggests our sample represents all levels of novelty, technology, complexity, and pace as follows:

- Novelty: eight derivative, 21 platform, 10 breakthrough;
- Technology: six low, 12 medium, 12 high, nine super-high;
- Complexity: two assembly, 16 system, 21 array; and
- Pace: 13 regular, 14 fast, 11 time-critical, one blitz

Chapter 2

Key Characteristics of Government Projects and Programs

In this section, six key characteristics of government projects and programs have been identified and discussed:

- Pursuing non-financial benefits;
- Being susceptible to political environment and dynamics;
- Following a mandated project management process;
- Being a large and complex megaproject;
- Having a long product life cycle; and
- Dealing with multiple stakeholders

It is important to establish an overall framework for the key characteristics, as these fit well with government projects and programs.

2.1 Non-Financial Benefits

Government projects are designed for different purposes than those of private sector projects. Whereas private sector projects are driven by profit maximization and return on investment, government projects are not-for-profit and managed to make efficient use of tax resources, and increase social and democratic values, such as equality, openness, and transparency.

Traditional measurement of project success is based on the "triple constraints" of time, cost, and scope. However, these relatively narrow constraints do not reflect other subjective or intangible considerations that can have a big impact on the perception of project success. Other success criteria have been proposed to supplement the conventional constraints for better project success measurement including organizational and project benefits (Zwikael & Smyrk, 2011). Project benefits represent performance improvements that contribute to the achievement of organizational objectives (Office of Government Commerce, 2007).

Government projects often have major non-financial benefits. They are undertaken in the service of the public (for the public good), rather than being driven by revenue or profit. For example, one benefit realized from the National Security Hotline project in Australia was increased reporting of suspicious behavior by members of the public, which contributed to the higher level strategic goal of enhancing national security. Another example of a non-financial benefit from a government project is the ANCOR system (CrimTrac project in Australia) aimed to enhance child safety by providing a nationally consistent approach to child offender registration and in some instances, enable police to case-manage registered sex offenders. Similarly, the Homeowner Insulation Program was designed to generate economic stimulus and support jobs and small business, as well as improving the energy efficiency of Australian homes.

2.2 Political Environment

Projects evolve around the preferences and expectations of owners. Owners of public projects could be more focused on political aspects and outcomes of projects and not necessarily coincide with realities of related industries or sectors. For instance, only 5% of more than 600 legislators in Washington have professional experience in construction and design industries (Lancaster, 2001), whereas construction sector and investments are generally considered as key drivers of economic growth. This lack of knowledge and expertise on how to manage a project and what to expect throughout the project life cycle, as well as political concerns in the limelight, possible short-term changes in management, and political risks, inevitably all have adverse effects on government projects.

Considering durations between elections in democratic regimes, government projects that are ruled by political agendas reflect relatively short-term views of legislators and ministers. Governments win elections with promises, creating expectations in voters, followers, the public, and other involved parties. Therefore, governments primarily target fulfilling their engagements to create sympathy and eventually win re-election. Policy makers are empowered by parliament or senate votes. Moreover, governments include motivated individuals in various ministries, who are pursuing progress in their political careers. In a world of limited resources, a certain level of competition for supplies, assets, or authority between these people and their respective departments is inevitable (Boyd & Chinyio, 2006), and government projects are no exception to that.

Government projects are affected by political risks in addition to well-known universal project risks and contingencies, due to several uncertain conditions. However, although political risk is a factor, the primary risks and uncertainties of government projects are related to the instabilities and dangers adversely influencing project finances or even threatening existence of the projects. These factors include nationalization of project assets, failed government grants or permits, tax or tariff increases, law changes, strikes, and terrorism (Bueno, 2010).

Regardless of political or other environmental factors, governments invest in many areas such as construction, IT, transportation, and security and defense, in order to spark economic stimulus. Through creation of buildings and infrastructure that support all other economic activities, governments ultimately pursue resource utilization, continuity of work, productivity, and performance. However, political environment is a significant factor of project success.

2.3 Formal Processes

The mandatory use of a formal process makes the management of government projects rather unique. This includes the formality and intensity of processes for budgeting, project planning and execution, project monitoring and control, project governance, and internal audits and reviews.

Government projects must follow strict budgeting processes, standards, and procedures that are unique to government agencies. The use of different types of funds and budget codes create complexity in the budgeting process, and fiscal year budgeting makes the management of government projects challenging. After approval, budgeted funds must be spent within that fiscal year with the minimum allowance of money carried over.

In addition to strict budgeting processes, government projects must follow standard processes for specific activities related to project management. For example, for acquisition activities, the projects within the U.S. Department of Defense (DOD) must follow the procedure for the Joint Capabilities Integration and Development System. The U.S. Federal Highway Administration (FHWA) planners, engineers, realty, and finance staff conduct reviews of state Department of Transportation (DOT) actions and processes to assure compliance with federal laws and regulations. These process reviews are evaluations of the state DOT management of its highway program under state and federal laws and regulations. For project monitoring and control, strict guidelines and procedures must be followed. In the U.S., EVM principle is strongly recommended for a project over $20 million, and it is mandatory for a project of more than $50 million for project monitoring and control. In addition, formal milestones must be established, and gatekeepers must be assigned.

While a certain set of standard formal project management processes should be practiced, ineffective use of processes has been found. This includes requirement elicitation process (ANAO, 2007) and risk management processes (GAO, 2005) among others. Because EVM is not a mandatory requirement by the Australian government, there have been some challenges in project monitoring and control for Australian government projects (ANAO, 2006).

Unique to government projects are the required strict internal audits and review processes. These include audits from the U.S. GAO, the NAO in the UK, and the ANAO. While the audit and review processes can identify problems, the intensity and frequency of audits can hamper project progress and the performance of the project personnel.

2.4 Megaprojects

A key characteristic of government projects and programs is that they fit into the category of "megaprojects." The United States Federal Highway Administration defines megaproject as "projects that cost more than $1 billion, or projects of a significant cost that attract a high level of public attention or political interests because of substantial direct and indirect impacts on the community environment and budget" (Capka, 2004). Merrow et al. (1988) also defined megaprojects as those whose capital cost exceeds $1 billion, although he used a cut-off value of $500 million in his study.

Risks and uncertainties associated with planning and implementing the project should be identified, analyzed, and incorporated during the planning phase in order to achieve commonly accepted criteria of a successful project, such as meeting project cost. Schedule is another key factor to include when discussing the megaproject. The typical length of a mega-project is more than 5 years. When it involves large programs, the duration can easily be doubled or tripled. Duration of government projects, in particular, can be affected significantly by dealing with multiple stakeholders, adopting appropriate technologies that are compatible and exchangeable for future usage, and managing change orders.

Conducting a thorough feasibility study, including benefit-cost analysis, during the initiation and planning phases and modularizing projects into smaller pieces can alleviate potential risks of high cost and long duration, as well as adapting to potential changes and uncertainties. Planning and coordination of suppliers and subcontractors are equally important and critical to keep the project on time and on budget as the impact could be significant to the overall project performance. Additionally, inefficient allocation of resources, underestimating project complexity and cost, competing management styles, and lack of leadership, can all contribute to poor performance.

A majority of the government megaprojects that we investigated did not meet the original scope, budget, or timeline. This resulted in stakeholder displeasure, additional cost to taxpayers, and other consequences. Poor project management performance of megaprojects has been attributed to too many stakeholders; lack of clear project governance structure, organizational structure, and timelines; and communication issues with competing interests. These factors resulted in reduced scope, increased expenditure, or in some instances, cancellation of projects.

2.5 Long Product Life Cycle

A long product/deliverable life cycle is another unique characteristic of government projects. The deliverable/outcome of government projects, including infrastructures, aircraft, and information systems, are expected to be operational for many years if not decades after completion. With the expectation that the product will have a long life, product design and planning can become very challenging. The product should be designed with the focus on quality and product life cycle in mind. The issues of product durability, functionality, and flexibility to address current and future needs are extremely important in government projects.

In addition to product quality, the anticipation of future needs can lead to a high level of technological uncertainty involved in product design. With a high level of technological uncertainty, decisions to adopt certain technologies become extremely challenging. If there are conventional technologies ready for adoption, the project team has to justify whether or not those technologies will become obsolete in the near future and whether or not the existing technologies are flexible enough to incorporate future changes. Using potentially obsolete technologies can shorten product life cycle, and decrease return on investment. Conversely, the evidence from this research also showed that in many cases advanced technologies required by the project did not even exist at the beginning of the project. The project team had to develop technologies along with the product, and in many cases, the technologies were not mature enough to be adopted, resulting in project failures.

2.6 Multiple Stakeholders

Each government project includes several stakeholders with various objectives and expectations, which require serious consideration during the planning and management processes.

Dealing with multiple parties is common in project management; however, multiple stakeholders who may affect the progress of the project in political, social, or financial ways, are a unique characteristic of government projects. After project stakeholders are recognized, distinguishing the potential purpose and impact of each involved party is of vital importance for project success. Although it may be difficult to identify agendas of multiple stakeholders, it can be advantageous to understand who is for or against the success of the project (Egeland, 2009). Considering the aforementioned political environment and related parties, planning for and management of stakeholders becomes a crucial factor in government projects. Namely "stakeholder engagement" is a useful "process of identifying key stakeholders, analyzing their influence on the project, and managing their influence and impact—including winning their support where possible" (DPAC, 2011). Key stakeholders in government projects are those individuals or groups whose interest in the project must be recognized if the project is to be successful—in particular, those stakeholders who will be positively or negatively affected during the project or on successful completion of the project. Non-key stakeholders are those individuals or groups identified as having a stake in the project but who do not necessarily influence its outcome (DPAC, 2011).

Who are the stakeholders in government projects? How should they be classified and described? The Australian Tasmanian Government Department of Premier and Cabinet (DPAC) classifies key stakeholders in government projects under five groups: review, related projects, outcome impacted, output utilization, and outcome accountable (DPAC, 2011). (1) Review stakeholders are groups or organizations that need to review or audit the project and its outputs or outcomes, such as quality review consultants and the budget committee. (2) The related projects group consists of projects and change activities that are likely to either have an impact on or be internally or externally impacted by the project. (3) Outcome impacted includes individuals, groups, organizations, and related projects that are potentially under positive or negative influence of project outcomes. Project beneficiaries will enjoy advancements in service, thanks to the project outcomes in question; whereas those that are negatively impacted may face possible forfeiture. (4) Output utilization parties are needed to realize project outcomes while using project outputs, such as business owners and project customers. Finally, (5) outcome accountability classes define responsible parties for the project's success, including corporate clients and project sponsors. As an essential stakeholder of government projects, citizens and communities may be considered under more than one of the aforementioned groups, in accordance with their relation to the project.

Alignment, collaboration, and communication among the stakeholders are issues to be addressed in every project. Multiple parties often are involved in government projects, including agencies, authorities, administrative personnel, and lobbyists. Project progress is dictated by not only alignment under political agendas but also formalized communication and collaboration channels. When government projects involve multiple agencies, forming cross-agency cooperation and establishing interagency agreements are of utmost importance for affluent project processes. In addition, engagement and collaboration among key personnel of possible critical activities such as procurement and acquisitions, planning and management, manufacturing (or production) and logistics, and marketing and sales significantly contributes to the success of the project.

Since government projects are mostly utilized as economic stimuli and public development tools, it is important to coordinate with existing operations and the related business community. To illustrate, an inner-city transportation project should be planned without creating any traffic congestion or other social and/or economic outcomes, if possible. Also, as the project progresses, its effects on current sewage and drainage infrastructure should be minimized with proper planning. Moreover, to increase the effectiveness of project outcomes, the production process of government projects should be tailored to consider the needs and requests of public and private parties who may be impacted by the project. Consultation from associated business communities could potentially sustain the usability of project products.

A basic physics experiment shows that an object under several forces moves in the direction of the resultant force of the components. Consider component forces pulling the object in different directions, with opposing forces acting on the object. If all forces draw the object in the same direction, then it moves under the total impulse of the components. Projects can be considered the object in this experiment, and if individual stakeholders try to "win" for themselves in the project, thus creating resistance in the overall "force," the project success would inevitably suffer. Conversely, if all involved parties work toward the same goal with alignment, coordination, and collaboration, project success may be achieved more easily than anticipated. Moreover, the identification of individual stakeholders and their respective purposes in a government project is of great importance to its ultimate success.

Chapter 3

Recommendations for Government Projects and Programs

In this section, 28 key recommendations for government projects and programs are discussed. These recommendations are grouped into six categories: non-financial benefits; political environment; formal process; megaprojects; long product life cycle; and multiple stakeholders.

3.1 Non-Financial Benefits

3.1.1 Identify Clear Non-Financial Benefits in the Business Case

All projects have clear efficiency targets, such as consideration of time and cost. However, the evaluation of project success cannot rely only upon performance in efficiency measures, but should also include assessment of the benefits realized from the project. For this reason, it is important to ensure target benefits are set before the project is approved and are included as part of the business case or project proposal.

Target benefits should be defined in a unique, specific, and measurable way to avoid potential mismanagement. To meet this requirement, target benefits should have a clear title and description, and be explicitly defined with a baseline and target value. Target benefits should also be measurable to allow managers to determine whether they have been realized. This suggests that target benefits should have agreed measures, a clear and relevant unit of measurement, a clear source of data, and be consistent with those measuring similar project benefits across the organization.

The UK government (OGC, 2007) outlines four steps in formulating target benefits of proposed projects: (1) identify the benefits, (2) select objective measures that reliably prove the benefits, (3) collect the baseline measure, and (4) decide how, when, and by whom the benefit measures will be collected.

A good project case that demonstrates the importance of including clear target benefits in the business case is the UK Benefit Card project. In May 1996, the Benefits Agency of the UK Department of Social Security and Post Office Counters Ltd. (the purchasers), jointly awarded a contract to Pathway, a subsidiary of the ICL computer services group. The Benefits Payment Card project was intended to replace the existing paper-based methods of paying social security benefits across Great Britain and Northern Ireland by 1999. The project involved introducing a magnetic stripe payment card, and automating the national network of post offices through which most benefits are paid. By 1999, the project had experienced considerable difficulties and it was decided that the benefits card system should be stopped. The computerized system for the Post Office was continued, eventually, was rolled out, and has been a success.

The project scope included automation of Post Office Counters Ltd.'s transactions for other customers, as well as its products and support processes. Target project benefits included improved competitiveness, increased efficiency, and enhanced commercial opportunities. The computerized system provided a virtually fraud-free, automated method of paying benefits at post offices; it enabled full and speedy reconciliation of benefits payments with recognized and accepted accounting practices; and it provided an improved service to both purchasers. In 1992, a study was initiated to identify the cheapest way to provide Benefit Books to Benefit Claimants, and it was discovered that a statistical method was available that could be used to quantify the level of fraudulent claims. However, this information was never used in the project case study and its implementation. A key recommendation of this project report was to establish clear and complete business case for projects.

3.1.2 Ensure that Target Benefits are Realistic and Achievable

The target benefits set for a proposed project should be realistic and achievable. The attainability of target benefits is important, as it can influence the commitments and actions undertaken. Similar to organizational goals, project goals should be challenging, yet realistic within the context and constraints of the organization. If target benefits are not attainable, the project team may lose its motivation and confidence in the project. This will impact the way stakeholders, customers, and senior managers view the project. A good case study to highlight this topic is the FiReControl project in the United Kingdom.

The FiReControl project was designed to improve the resilience, efficiency, and technology of the Fire and Rescue Service by replacing 46 local control rooms with a network of nine purpose-built regional control centers using a national computer system to handle calls, mobilize equipment, and manage incidents. The department considered a number of options before making its decision. It estimated that continuing with FiReControl would cost £390 million but delivery would be delayed by another year to May 2012. In comparison, the cost of cancelling the project and upgrading local control rooms was estimated to be between £310 and £400 million. Because of uncertainty over delivery and associated additional costs of FiReControl, the department decided to terminate the contract and project. A key recommendation from this project is to ensure that expected costs/benefits and timetables are realistic.

3.1.3 Establish an Agreed-Upon Evaluation Methodology for Project Benefits

A visible and documented formal process with clearly defined stages and gates is beneficial to project success. The use of a formal benefit formulation process varies across public agencies. In some government agencies, a formal process was simply unavailable, while in others it was either embedded in existing budgeting and costing systems, or under development.

The balanced scorecard is a well-known and popular tool for this purpose. There are generally four dimensions to the scorecard: growth/innovation, internal processes, and customer and financial perspectives. Although the name or the number of dimensions may change, it is critical that management identify the dimensions that contribute to the successful implementation and monitoring of the project. Barclay (2008) proposed a project performance scorecard that contains five dimensions: project process, benefit use, quality, innovation/ learning, and stakeholder. The Digital Education Revolution (DER) project in Australia clearly demonstrates the importance of having a formal benefit formulation process.

The Australian National Secondary School Computer Fund (NSSCF) is helping schools and school systems to provide new computers and other information and communication technology (ICT) equipment for students. The fund was established to achieve a computer to student ratio of 1:1 for students in Years 9 to 12 by the end of 2011. Three application-based funding rounds took place in 2008 and 2009, with $295 million in funding provided to schools in need. The government has also commenced provision of an additional $1.1 billion in funding to education authorities on a per capita basis for schools to achieve and sustain a computer to student ratio of 1:1. Through the NSSCF, the Australian government provided funding of $1,000 per computer and up to $1,500 for the installation and maintenance of each device.

Education authorities have reported solid progress to date in the installation of computers purchased using NSSCF funding, indicating 97% of schools achieved the computer to student ratio of 1:2 in Round 1, and 80% of schools achieved the 1:2 ratio in Rounds 2 and 2.1, before the deadline. More than 434,000 computers had been installed by the target date. A survey of school principals showed a positive impact on teaching and learning, with students becoming more engaged due to their increased access to computers.

A key recommendation from the DER project is to establish an agreed-upon evaluation methodology for the project. Earlier investment in evaluation methodologies and associated data as the program evolved would have provided a stronger foundation for measuring the impact of the DER project, particularly given the proposed focus of the evaluation on the four strands of change: leadership, infrastructure, learning resources, and teacher capability.

3.1.4 Evaluate the Impact of the Project on the Achievement of Strategic Goals

Long-term orientation is the tendency to prioritize the long-range implications and impact of decisions and actions that come to fruition after an extended time period. Organizations with a greater consensus on mission, such as a police force, fire department, public works department, or other public organization, may be more inclined to engage in strategic management than those experiencing intense conflict within the governing body, or within the executive staff. A public agency's value system, organizational culture, leadership style, management capacity, and analytical capabilities, as well as its exposure and quality of experience with strategic planning and management are all likely to determine its ability to engage in effective strategic planning and management. The importance of linking project performance measurement and targets to strategic organizational goals by having a long-term orientation of projects is demonstrated by the U.S. Navy Marine Corps Intranet (NMCI) project.

The NMCI project was a multiyear IT services program. Project goals were to provide information superiority—an uninterrupted information flow, and the ability to exploit or deny an adversary's ability to do the same—and to foster innovative ways of operating through interoperable and shared network services. The Navy awarded the NMCI services contract—valued at $9.3 billion—to Electronic Data Systems (EDS) in October 2000. The contract calls for EDS to replace thousands of independent networks, applications, and other hardware and software with a single, internal communications network (intranet), and associated desktop, server, and infrastructure assets and services for Navy and Marine Corps customers (end users, network operators, and commanders).

The Navy's three groups of NMCI customers report varied levels of satisfaction with the program, but collectively these customers generally are not satisfied. With respect to end users, the Navy reports that overall satisfaction with NMCI improved between 2003 and 2005; however, reported satisfaction levels have dropped since September 2005. While the Navy reports that the overall level of end-user satisfaction with contractor provided services has averaged about 76% since April 2004, this is below the Navy-wide target of 85% and includes many survey responses at the lower end of the range that the Navy has defined as "satisfied." Commanders and network operations leaders generally are not satisfied with NMCI. In addition, officials representing each of the customer groups at five shipyard or air depot installations expressed a number of concerns and areas of dissatisfaction with NMCI. Without satisfied customers, the Navy runs the risk that NMCI will not attain the widespread acceptance necessary to achieve strategic program goals. NMCI has not met its two strategic goals—to provide information superiority and to foster innovation via interoperability and shared services. The Navy's mapping shows that NMCI has met only three of 20 performance targets (15%). This means that the mission-critical information superiority and operational innovation outcomes used to justify NMCI have yet to be attained.

A key recommendation from the NMCI project was to ensure that adopting robust performance management practices should include evaluating and appropriately adjusting the original plan for measuring achievement of strategic program goals.

3.2 Political Environment

3.2.1 Consider Legal Consultation to Ensure that Proposed Ideas are in Line with Current Legislation

Large public projects are often planned and built in complicated and changing political environments. It is important to ensure the proposed ideas are in line with current legislation before moving forward with a product. Legal consultation is recommended as a useful and effective way to accomplish this. The CrimTrac project provides an example.

During the 1998 Australian federal election campaign, the Federal Coalition pledged $50 million over three years to establish the CrimTrac Agency as part of its Safer and Stronger

Australia policy to support and enhance a national crime prevention environment. The agency achieves this through the specification, development, delivery, and maintenance of modern, high-quality, rapid access, electronic police information services, and investigative tools for the provision of criminal history checking services to accredited third-party agencies. The program was scheduled for installation within 20 months but it was successfully completed in 18 months. The CrimTrac Agency began operational and acceptance testing in March 2001, and the system was accepted on April 30, 2001, which was a major milestone. As part of the initiative, the National Automated Fingerprint Identification System Program developed the most effective system within the $20.3 million budget.

Major potential issues associated with the project included governance, oversight problems, decision making, and information sharing difficulties. The legislative complexities between jurisdictions have restricted the ability of the National Criminal Investigation DNA Database of Australia to perform inter-jurisdictional matching. Difficulties exist in aligning the legislation and slow progress has been achieved in establishing cross-jurisdictional matching arrangements. Moreover, there were difficulties in gaining a formal agreement from police jurisdictions to share and match DNA information in accordance with individual jurisdictional legislative requirements.

In addition, the National Child Sex Offender System (NCSOS) was established in June 2002 and in November 2003 the Australian National Child Offender Register (ANCOR) was created as a replacement to NCSOS. ANCOR launched in September 2004 and annually updated until September 2006. The post-implementation review for ANCOR was conducted in 2006 after it achieved full functionality. Although ANCOR originally was scheduled for use between November 2003 and July 2004, the program continued to September 2006 due to legislative amendments.

A major delay in the CrimTrac project occurred because systems were being developed that did not align with current Australian laws. For government projects, such as CrimTrac, the existing body of law should be closely examined to prevent further confusion and problems throughout the project duration or after the completion. No project is undertaken for unfruitful and incommodious end products. Hence, pre-project alignment is of utmost significance for a successful, productive project.

3.2.2 Consider Financial Consultation to Improve Understanding of Economic Aspects of the Project

Financial consultation can provide the management expertise to translate economic aspects of megaprojects. Combined with monetary expertise, risk assessment and financial analysis can help reduce financial risks and ensure that projects operate smoothly. The following case study on the Channel Tunnel between England and France demonstrates the importance of financial consultation.

The Channel Tunnel, also known as the Chunnel, is a 31.4-mile undersea rail tunnel linking Folkestone, Kent, England, with Coquelles, Pas-de-Calais, near Calais in northern France, beneath the English Channel at the Strait of Dover. At its lowest point, it is 75 meters (250 ft.) deep. At 23.5 miles, the Channel Tunnel possesses the longest undersea portion of any tunnel in the world, although the Seikan Tunnel in Japan is both longer overall at 33.5 miles, and deeper at 240 meters (790 ft.) below sea level. The tunnel carries high-speed Eurostar passenger trains, Eurotunnel Shuttle roll-on/roll-off vehicle transport—the largest in the world—and international rail freight trains. The tunnel connects end-to-end with the LGV Nord and High Speed 1 railway lines. In 1996, the American Society of Civil Engineers identified the tunnel as one of the Seven Wonders of the Modern World. Construction of the tunnel started in 1988; the project took approximately 20% longer than planned (6 years vs. 5 years) and came in 80% over budget (4.6 billion pounds vs. 2.6 billion pound forecast).

Delays mainly resulted from three factors: (1) changed specifications for the tunnel due to the need for air conditioning systems to improve safety that were not part of the initial design; (2) poor communication between the British and French teams who were essentially tunneling from the two different sides and meeting in the middle; (3) competing firms bid on the project, which may have resulted in the 'winner's curse' of the successful bidders having the lowest and most optimistic price estimates. Financial problems with the Channel Tunnel were caused by overly optimistic revenue projections, on top of construction cost overruns. Even if the target cost arrangements in place forced all participants (client, Rail Link Engineering (RLE), and the individual construction contractors) to bear some financial risk, improper cost management and lack of financial consultation inevitably caused poor economic project outcomes. As a consequence of the financial exposure both to the client and RLE, project managers have developed and implemented an active risk management program, encompassing both qualitative and quantitative processes.

Eurotunnel was not able to revisit or fundamentally modify this design. It simply had to try to control and manage project costs and configuration during the 7-year construction program. This proved to be very difficult. The Independent Safety Authority, which was created by the governments, imposed significant constraints on the design and made up the rules as it went along, imposing more and more onerous and costly requirements on the project. This was an unusual arrangement since the safety design standards typically are known in advance for most projects. It was inevitable in this case, because of the unique characteristics of the project, and was another risk that had to be accepted by the financiers. Eurotunnel did not properly understand the economics of its competitors, the ferries, and their potential to drastically reduce their prices while remaining profitable. It was not realized at that time that freight lorries would prove to be the most profitable market, requiring a switch of emphasis from the passenger shuttle over time.

The Chunnel project would have benefitted from the financial management expertise of experienced consultants in order to understand the economic aspects of megaproject management. The project suffered significantly due to a lack of risk assessment, financial projection analysis, and monetary expertise. Thus, appointment of or even consultation with a financial expert may have minimized or prevented the effects of revealed problematic issues.

3.2.3 Ensure that the Project is Aligned with Agencies' Strategies

It is recommended that government projects, especially those with long duration and large budgets, are planned to align with existing agencies' strategies. To achieve project success, project characteristics such as scope, cost, schedule, capability, performance, and quality should meet desired levels to reflect those strategies. The AIR87 project demonstrates the importance of project alignment with strategies.

Project AIR87 was proposed to improve Australian Army Aviation with the acquisition of Armed Reconnaissance Helicopter (ARH) capability 22 Eurocopter Tiger helicopters, including a fully instrumented ARH, a training system consisting of a Full Flight and Mission Simulator; two Cockpit Procedures Trainers; and ground crew training devices. Other supporting components included the ARH Software Support Capability, a Ground Mission Management System to support operational communications, Electronic Warfare Mission Support System, a Maintenance Management System, facilities, and ammunition.

The project was planned for completion within 120 months, whereas it was only possible for the project to reach full operating capability with a one-year delay and in 132 months. Despite numerous delays, the project seemed to be successful and was completed within the $2 billion budget. Successful initial operation of 21 of the 22 helicopters was achieved; however, the helicopters were not deployed to Afghanistan until February 2012 because of delay in the delivery of night-vision helmets.

A review report on the project stated that:

> [Department of] Defence has often pursued a unique Australian solution, or modified an existing solution, without appropriate understanding of the attendant risks to cost, schedule and delivery. It is important that this be avoided in the future. While project requirements must ultimately reflect the demands of operational performance, they need to be tempered by the realities of cost, risk and what the market can deliver off-the-shelf and otherwise. Unless this is done, informed decisions about the appropriate mix of cost, schedule, risk and capability are impossible. (Mortimer Review, 2008, p. 17)

Therefore, the Public Defence Capability Plan should have contained sufficient information on project scope and timing to enable development of strategic business plans. Moreover, the explicit cost bands presently disclosed should have been replaced by a measure relative to the Defence Materiel Organisation Acquisition Category framework.

3.2.4 Consider Public-Private Partnership (PPP) when Appropriate

Public-private partnerships (PPPs) are vital to the development of social and economic aspects of large government projects. PPP refers to a variety of alternative arrangements for government projects that transfer more of the risk associated with and control of a project to a private partner. Among the most extensive public-private partnerships are those in which a private firm provides financing for a project, and designs and builds it, in exchange for the right to operate and maintain it over its useful life. The most common type of PPP, however, is the more limited "design-build" agreement in which one contractor agrees to both design and build a project rather than having the public sector manage each of those steps independently. More risks are transferred to the contractor than would be under the traditional approach. The downside of transferring the risk and control of a project to a private firm is that it may limit the government's ability to respond to changing conditions or to achieve other objectives that might benefit tax payers. PPP has been widely applied in infrastructure projects. A possible application could be in the following U.S. Department of Defense (DOD) projects.

The U.S. Secretary of Defense recommended specific military installations for realignment and closure to achieve fiscal efficiencies or savings of $36 billion by 2025. The Defense Authorization Amendments and Base Realignment and Closure (BRAC) Act became public law in 1988 and were scheduled to end in September 1995, although delays extended the completion date to September 15, 2011. Due to the delays, the project surpassed the original budget of $35 billion reaching $57.1 billion. Overall, the U.S. government was satisfied with the outcome of the BRAC process and its product to realign or close military base operations, as well as to achieve greater cost efficiency and savings. After each round of BRAC, the U.S. government holds independent reviews and then presents recommendations for future BRAC. For example, the DOD has created an improved selection ranking system.

On the other hand, major problems in the project included poor planning and lack of control over cost, risk, and quality management. DOD tried to complete the entire BRAC project with in-house operational capabilities. In fact, lessons learned from the earlier BRACs were not effectively applied. The project suffered greatly without the help of valuable and applicable experiences. Although every BRAC operation is not exactly the same, it is clear that similar processes should be applied to different base locations.

Thus, it is suggested to not only monitor actual costs and savings with a better DOD financial management system, but also spend more time conducting cost analyses for better decisions, shorter time periods, quality standards determined by all stakeholders, and better resource management of civilian and military personnel at DOD facilities that undergo BRAC. PPP should be utilized whenever appropriate throughout the BRAC process to increase project performance. Trying to complete the entire operation with in-house project tools, but without utilizing seasoned private sector parties has proved to be pointless and unsuccessful. BRACs and government projects in general would benefit significantly from the expertise of private parties, when appropriate.

3.2.5 Ensure PPPs are Economically Feasible

Ensuring that PPPs are economically feasible is critical. The New South Wales M7 Motorway project in New South Wales, Australia, is a successful example.

The M7 Motorway was constructed under a Build Own Operate Transfer (BOOT) contract model and was established as a PPP. The main contractor was the Westlink Motorway consortium, which included road constructors Abigroup and Leighton Contractors; tolling and customer management operator Transurban; and motorway investor Macquarie Infrastructure Group. This consortium structure was unique at the time, being the first to include a tolling and customer management operator as an equity investor. Working in a joint venture, Maunsell and SMEC were lead consultants for the engineering design. The motorway continues to be maintained by Leighton Contractors and Bilfinger Berger consortium, which will operate the motorway until February 2037, when it will be transferred to the government. The allowed time for construction was 42.5 months; however, contractors were able to complete it in less than 3 years (34 months). In addition, electronic tolling facilities were available 10 months sooner than anticipated. In spite of the early completion, construction costs were $15 million over the budgeted $1.5 billion, due to client specified changes. The total project costs including construction, connecting road works, and financing, was estimated at $2.2 billion.

An overall steering committee and a review panel, both made up of representatives from state and commonwealth governments, were established to oversee the M7 project. This allowed the state and commonwealth governments to be informed on the progress and activities, generating a sense of ownership. The governance of the project was established contractually by the project deed between the Roads and Traffic Authority (RTA) and the project company. The project deed sets out governance and obligations over the life of the project, including the operating term. This structure is often absent from other procurement models that focus only on the construction phase.

Overall, the scope of project management in the M7 Motorway may be superior to other government projects, mostly because of the PPP arrangements. The site and the works had to be broken down into manageable portions, with each portion appropriately resourced, to ensure uniform controls. Communications were established across the whole site. An umbrella management overlay was installed to ensure that uniformity of approach was maintained across the project. The project team consciously broke this scope down to manageable portions and adopted a "stretch target" ethos for those components to ensure that the team was not overwhelmed by the scale and time objectives were maintained. Analysis demonstrated that the motorway could be commercially viable as a toll road. By utilizing PPP in development of a toll road, the infrastructure delivery could be accelerated, with appropriate risk transfer, as opposed to a potentially long delay while waiting for budget headroom for government funding. The BOOT model provides inherent benefits to government by allocating risk to the private sector. Under this model, government can transfer the significant risks of toll road construction, tolling operations, and traffic forecasts to the contractors from the private sector. While there have been issues with the transfer of patronage risk with other toll roads, this project demonstrates that patronage risk can be successfully transferred when the need for the road is clear, as demonstrated by robust demand forecasting rather than by "gaps on maps" or congestion.

3.2.6 Provide Project Managers More Authority

The Bell Boeing V-22 Osprey is an American multi-mission, Tiltrotor military aircraft with both vertical takeoff and landing, and short takeoff and landing capability. It is designed to combine the functionality of a conventional helicopter with the long-range, high-speed cruise performance of a turboprop aircraft. The program began in December 1981 and was originally scheduled to be completed in 1984. With multiple delays and scope changes, the completion date was extended three times to 1985, 1986, and finally to 2016 (Conahan, 1986). The initial program budget was $88.6 million, however with postponements, the budget increased to $188.5 million (1985), grew to $580 million (1986), and finally reached $36.2 billion (2016) (Conahan, 1986). As of today, the program is still in progress with a reduced scope, which makes estimation of its progress unavailable. The V-22 originally was designed to perform various maneuvers. However, it was later discovered that due to the design, it was fundamentally impossible for it to perform certain actions, and the lack of additional research and testing resulted in the deaths of multiple pilots (Thompson, 2007). Additionally, the price/unit has continued to increase each year, and the expected total production has decreased (Conahan, 1986).

The project team comprised multiple groups/individuals, including the joint technology assessment group (Army, Navy, Air Force, Marines); outsourced contractors; the assigned program manager for approval of acquisition strategy, needed by the Chief of Naval Material; Army original executive service (later replaced by the Navy in December 1982); appointed contracting officers; members of the house and senate needed to confer and provide funding each year for the project; Defense Systems Review Council; and the Secretary of Defense, needed to approve full-scale development. Thus, the project involved collaborative efforts among multiple branches/organizations, and approval from high-ranking government officials for each stage, which may have resulted in inefficiencies (Conahan, 1986).

When government projects involve several political stakeholders with various agendas, providing more authority to the project manager may increase project efficiency, productivity, and eventually accomplishment. GAO (1986) asserts the following:

> The program manager's role is clear except in the military requirements area. Uncertain is whether the program manager has the latitude to ensure a flexibly stated requirement that encourages (1) a creative industry design process, (2) competition, and (3) reexamination of the requirement, as costs and other information become available. The program manager's role did not always conform to policy due to such reasons as late assignment to the program. Often, the program manager and the contracting officer did not operate as a team in planning

competitive strategies for new weapon system programs. The contracting officer is frequently not assigned early enough to be involved in acquisition strategy planning, nor is DOD policy clear on this role. In executing such plans, the contracting officer's role is clear in policy but diverges so widely in both practice and perception that it brings into question what the fundamental policy is or should be. (GAO, 1986, p. 3)

3.3 Formal Process

3.3.1 Establish and Follow Government Project Management Framework and Processes

This study revealed that some government agencies have formal processes which the project community must follow, while other government agencies do not require the same processes. For example, the procurement activities for projects funded by the U.S. DOD must follow the procedure for the Joint Capabilities Integration and Development System. Also, government agencies in different countries do not find the same level of significance in a certain process, tool, or technique. For example, EVM is required by projects sponsored by the DOD.

In general, government agencies must monitor the development of their project management capability, including project management processes. With the high degree of complexity, the government project must follow formal project management processes. Government specific processes must be developed, and each government agency should be able to adapt its processes contingent to its projects.

3.3.2 Follow Formal Planning and Estimating Processes that Incorporate Lessons Learned

Government projects must follow formal planning and estimating processes. However, some government agencies do not have such a process. For example, lack of a formal planning and estimating process was evident in the Secure Border Initiative Network Project

(SBInet) of the U.S. Department of Homeland Security (DHS). The mission of SBInet is to enhance and improve border security by identifying, designing, developing, deploying, and maintaining border security tools, capabilities, and other systems; establish a bridge between operational and acquisition elements in U.S. Customs and Border Protection to ensure deployed technologies provide the needed capabilities; and provide program management expertise and acquisition competency for implementing and executing nationally significant border security programs. Problems with project scope, represented in the Work Breakdown Structure, caused project delays as well as accountability issues with contractors. Lack of a project master schedule at the beginning of the project resulted in problems with project scope and time. Without the master schedule, the project teams followed a task/order-specific baseline, resulting in unnecessary task concurrency that increased project risks. Because SBInet did not have a clear schedule, the oversight of the project's progress was difficult and led to an overall lack of accountability for the project.

This case example demonstrates the necessity for formal planning and estimating processes. Such processes lay a foundation for development of a high quality project planning document. In addition to the formal processes, lessons learned should be considered during the planning and estimating. The success or failure from previous projects should be considered and applied. Given that the knowledge and lessons learned do exist within each government agency or within the industry in general, to promote the use of lessons learned, more focus should be put toward the dissemination and adaptation of the knowledge to the government personnel.

3.3.3 Follow a Formal Risk Management Process

In managing government projects, it is important to establish a formal and standard risk management process. The process should include risk identification, risk assessment (qualification and quantification), risk handling (response planning), risk surveillance (monitoring and control), and risk closure. Risk management is not new to government projects, and historically, it has been practiced rigorously in many government projects. Risk identification must be ongoing as new risks can emerge throughout the project, and the impact and probability of each risk should be assessed. Risks should be used as a basis for subsequent management and contingency planning. A risk manager should be assigned to track and respond to each risk. In some cases, an independent auditor or a risk scrutinizer should be assigned to monitor how risks are handled by the project team and to report such information to senior management on a regular basis. Closed risks should be retained in a closed risk register and reviewed on a regular basis to detect recurrence. However, despite these recommended best practices, many government projects are managed without a formal or proper risk management process, as shown in the example below.

The Benefits Payment Card (BPC) project, administered by the Department of Social Security Benefits Agency, is one example of issues that can arise when projects are managed without proper risk management practices (NAO, 2000). BPC was initiated to replace the existing paper-based methods of distributing social security benefits with a magnetic stripe payment card, and to automate the national network of post offices through which most benefits are paid across Great Britain and Northern Ireland. BPC was considered a high-risk project. Although the BPC project team practiced risk identification, there was difficulty in distributing the risk register to all involved parties so that the risks could be fully and appropriately considered and addressed. Thus, a shared and open approach to risk management across the entire project was not achieved, and the obligation and responsibility toward project risks were unclear.

3.3.4 Follow Formal Project Monitoring and Change Management Processes

Project monitoring can also affect the success of government projects. EVM is a proven concept for project monitoring that integrates scope, schedule, and cost measures to gauge project progress. Although many government projects have successfully implemented EVM, many others have not. The SBInet project provides an excellent example. Although EVM was employed to provide objective insight into project cost and schedule performance, EVM data was unreliable, and earned value performance was not adequately measured. This may be due to a lack of proper Work Breakdown Schedule and master schedule resulting in a negative impact on the project baseline.

Proper project monitoring will lead to proper project control and changes in the project. This demonstrates the necessity of a formal change management process. Because of the complexity of government projects, many changes are likely to occur as the project progresses. As illustrated by cases in this research, requirement changes can have negative impacts on project performance, and changes occurring in the later phases of the project can be detrimental to project objectives (Dvir & Lechler, 2004). Change decisions must be implemented with careful consideration. A formal change management process can facilitate the decision to implement changes and may help assure management that changes made are beneficial to the overall project objectives.

3.3.5 Establish and Follow Project Governance Framework

Governance is an important issue in managing government projects. The lack of management control and oversight resulted in poor performance of most of the projects cited. This issue was evident in the San Francisco Oakland Bay Bridge project. This project involved approximately seven miles of structure and included replacement of the east span (a 10,176-foot steel truss from Oakland to Yerba Buena Island) and retrofit of the west span from Yerba Buena Island to San Francisco. The bridge project had numerous project management problems, including lack of a high-level single point of authority. At times, responsibility appeared to be diffuse and undefined, and communication among units of the California Department of Transportation was poorly coordinated. The project clearly demonstrates the need for appropriate management controls and processes to increase project success.

An organization embarking on large-scale projects must ensure that it has established procedures and policies specifically for project governance. Management can establish an enterprise project management office to oversee all high priority projects. The office should have authority to establish and enforce standards for government projects. Standards may range from financial controls to governance and senior management oversight. Many cases in this study indicate that the lack of an experienced senior responsible owner (SRO) leads to poor project governance. Management should assign a project owner to ensure oversight and accountability and must ensure that the authority of the SRO is commensurate with his or her roles and responsibilities. The SRO may establish and empower a project office, which is dedicated to overarching project monitoring and control, provides support to the project teams, and serves as a formal channel to relay project information to the SRO and vice versa.

A project steering committee should be established to ensure the active involvement of senior management in the project. In addition, a formal auditing and reviewing process should be established. The auditors who are independent of the project team should be assigned to investigate the performance of the project and the project team, and to identify issues impacting performance. The auditor should provide project information and recommendations to senior management and the SRO for making proper project decisions. However, too many audits and reviews can distract project personnel from project activities, adversely affecting progress and performance. It was found in the FBI Trilogy program, which was intended to modernize the bureau's outdated information technology infrastructure, had undergone more than 100 investigations and audits in the IT area (National Research Council, 2004). While it was true that the performance of the project was seriously deficient, responding to such investigations and audits took the project team and management away from project work.

3.4 Megaprojects

3.4.1 Develop a Base Cost Estimate and Integrated Master Schedule (IMS) for Megaprojects

Front-end planning ensures proper managerial processes and enables project personnel to achieve targets. According to research conducted by Dvir et al. (2003), there is a significant positive relationship between project success and development efforts incorporated into the origination and initiation phases, including work on project goals and specifications. Many government projects and programs failed to adopt two fundamental project management techniques: base cost estimate and Integrated Master Schedule (IMS). The overall work breakdown structure of this project was not broken down into the product level, and not having an IMS resulted in insufficient risk assessment which led to inadequate schedule reserve time and thus overlaps in critical path activities. In the case of SBInet, the GAO specifically called for the secretary of DHS to direct the SBI executive director to improve DHS management and oversight of the prime contractor by establishing and validating "timely, complete, and accurate performance measurement" (GAO, 2010, p.42).

Government projects are especially susceptible to budget changes. Changes in the majority party can bring new emphasis to or scrutiny of your project. Programs with competing or overlapping objectives are more likely to be formed or elevated in importance. Good reporting and solid metrics are crucial to present a clear picture of the progress and benefits of your program or project. You may be accomplishing your program goals efficiently, but if the public doesn't see that and you can't prove it, your program will suffer the consequences. Therefore, establishing and monitoring performance based on established baselines is critical. While change is inevitable, with adequate tracking of baseline and progress changes can be managed with sensible measurement and enable more intelligent solutions powered by information. Ensuring adequate systems and processes are set up to manage program performance, issues, communications, and stakeholders will reduce tracking and analysis errors and enable timely reporting.

Establishing the IMS at project inception and engaging key operations staff throughout scheduling processes will help project managers track all the schedules, conduct proper risk management, coordinate acquisition management, and assist in personnel management. IMS should be broadly disseminated to the organization and audited regularly to keep track of the consumed resources. Both the 2010 Census program and DOD's Defense Integrated Military Human Resources System program failed to establish a clear integrated master schedule to work with from the project's initial phase.

3.4.2 Align the Project Cost with the Annual Budget Cycle

When possible, aligning project cost with the yearly budget cycle may be beneficial in making good strategic decisions for the government project. In the case of Australia's Project Air87, the chief financial officer should apply a defense capacity plan, including its impact on future personnel and operating costs, as part of annual project budget considerations. To achieve this, the auditing agency audits the cost and schedule estimations within the capability plan to ensure that the cost estimates are as practical and as accurate as possible. The capacity plan should contain sufficient information on project scope and timing to enable managers to develop strategic business plans, and the explicit cost bands presently disclosed should be replaced by a measure relative to the acquisition category framework.

3.4.3 Consider Off-the-Shelf Solutions over High-risk New Development When Possible

There is always temptation and a risk involved in developing completely new systems or solutions instead of trying to modify or build upon an existing solution for large acquisition projects. Functional and operational system requirements and specifications should be aligned and compared with off-the-shelf solutions. Uncertain elements including cost, schedule, and risks should be planned for and analyzed. In cases involving defense projects, a more conservative approach should be employed such as buying Military Off-The-Shelf (MOTS) equipment and solutions that do not require major development or extensive modification. The C-17 Globemaster and Boeing FA-18 Super Hornet acquisitions are examples of MOTS projects that were completed below budget and/or ahead of schedule. The standard acquisition cycle can be accelerated significantly when the major supplies being procured are off-the-shelf production items. However, accelerated establishment of support systems may be more difficult and should be addressed early by management.

3.4.4 Split Programs into Smaller Manageable Projects for Tight Project Control

When mega programs are complex, technologically advanced, and high risk, the management team should establish a central project management office to respond to the level of complexity and uncertainty. The most efficient way to plan and manage these projects is by modularizing the program into smaller projects based on the characteristics or technology applied to the deliverables. Breaking down the program to manageable deliverables will help the project team effectively monitor and control the project.

When managers apply state of the art technology to a very complex system, such as a megaproject, it is often very difficult to plan, manage, and deliver an expected product. In the case of the Joint Strike Fighter program, maintaining senior leadership's increased focus on program results, holding government and contractors accountable for improving performance, and greater attention to project budget may help limit future cost growth and the consequences for other programs in the portfolio.

3.4.5 Develop Contingency Plan and Monitor Risks

It is essential to set realistic project schedules for megaprojects with complex integrated systems. In particular, the contingency management plan and contingency reserve funding should be in place to provide a financial safeguard for project managers against the inherent uncertainties, risks, or unexpected events that may arise during the course of the project. Applying project management tools and techniques and employing risk management principles continuously to manage and adopt risks and uncertainties proactively will help ensure the success of megaprojects. Timely and effective risk identification, management, and response, and informing government officials and relevant stakeholders about potential risks and any updated mitigation strategies will help project managers better understand the level of inherent risk and potential consequences of realized risk in the program. Finally, compliance and audit programs should be operational at the beginning of the program and should reflect the program's requirements, including specific program risks associated with the operating environment and program participants.

3.4.6 Identify Training Needs for Large-Scale Megaprojects

Essential project management training is critical for team members as well as stakeholders of large-scale megaprojects. They should have basic information technology skills, and a basic understanding of data that are being measured and collected, and overall project management processes, tools, and techniques. Training should be structured and relevant, and use innovative means and modes for effective delivery.

3.5 Long Product Life Cycle

3.5.1 Ensure Robust Design and Quality Management Process

A long product life cycle requires careful product design and planning, including the adoption of technologies. To achieve high product quality for long-term utilization, the project team must have a robust product design, coupled with an effective quality management process. This is illustrated by the case of the Dallas Area Rapid Transit (DART), which was planned to build the Northwest/Southeast light rail transit extension. DART implemented a design-build process in which a single entity is responsible for both design and construction. This streamlined process promoted opportunities for creativity and innovation through the ongoing collaboration of the design and construction teams. It was through design-build efforts that the project team identified eight Alternative Technical Concepts (ATCs). The ATCs, approved and submitted as part of the bidding process, included concrete panels at roadway crossings and a cost-effective superstructure design. As part of an overall quality-controlled program, any changes to the design or construction plan must be reviewed and remain consistent with the specifications and design goals for the project.

3.5.2 Reduce the Use of Unapproved (too advanced) Technologies

To address future needs associated with achieving a long product life, a project team must consider the challenges of technology adoption. In many cases, the technologies did not exist at the beginning of the project. The project team may have had to develop new technologies along with development of the product. This is illustrated by the Future Combat System (FCS), funded by the U.S. DOD. This project plan included development of an advanced system of manned and unmanned ground and air vehicles. The vehicles were enabled to utilize a networked system of communications software that would allow uninterrupted connection with all systems on the battlefield and weigh 50% less than comparable existing systems. The goal was to make the Army lighter, more flexible, and ultimately more effective on the battlefield. The majority of the technologies intended for use in this project did not exist or were not mature when the project commenced. This caused a very high degree of uncertainty in development, testing, and integration of all new systems. Out of the 46 new technologies that were needed for the project, only one reached the required level of maturity. This in turn caused the project to fail.

The technological issues faced by the FCS project team perhaps were unavoidable since the project was very complex and in need of advanced technologies. If possible with other projects, the project team should avoid use of unapproved (too advanced) technologies. To alleviate the issue of technology obsolescence, the project team may consider a flexible design to accommodate the integration of future advanced technologies. The project team should consult with technology experts about trends and long-term technology changes. In addition, the project team should develop and implement a formal change management process.

3.6 Multiple Stakeholders

3.6.1 Engage Procurement Personnel on the Project Team

It is recommended that agencies match their acquisition approaches to product characteristics, which are the initial source of costs and risks. Acquisition for large complex projects is therefore both costly and risky, whether it is internal or contract. The successful acquisition of any complex product is a function of multiple steps, including contract design, contract management, and the "assembly vs. production" choice. The successful acquisition of a complex product requires both the purchasing agency and the vendor to work collaboratively to specify the product's attributes and performance requirements, and to invest in designing and building a specialized production process for product delivery. Although effective acquisition of complex products requires new policies and tools, prohibiting agencies from using more flexible acquisition approaches may result in a premature decision to utilize assembly functions before they have the capacity to do so, resulting in delivery delays and cost overruns. Policy makers should foster efforts to provide procurement personnel with more information rather than constrain contracting practices.

The U.S. Coast Guard's Deepwater program demonstrates the importance of engaging procurement personnel. Known as Project Deepwater, the program is a major long-term effort to upgrade and overhaul the Coast Guard's Deepwater sea and air vessels along with the command and control links among them.

The Coast Guard's multiple missions and global reach meant that its objectives varied from location to location and changed frequently. In the early 1990s, many of the Coast Guard's assets were not ideally suited to those modern missions. The Coast Guard needed to acquire a system of interoperable assets with seamless communication and coordination that could adapt quickly to changing circumstances in a decentralized decision-making environment. In 1998, Congress and the Clinton administration committed to a multi-year appropriation of $500 million/year to upgrade the Coast Guard's assets. Among three industry teams, the Coast Guard selected a system design from Integrated Coast Guard Systems (ICGS), which proposed to integrate Deepwater assets in a state-of-the-art command, control, communications, computers and intelligence, surveillance, and reconnaissance system.

The project consists of two phases. Phase 1 included design, construction, deployment, support, and integration of each individual component of Deepwater into a cohesive system. ICGS was charged with this phase, which started in June 2002 with the first 5-year Deepwater contract and finished by March 2007. During the second phase, starting in April 2007, the Coast Guard took over the lead role in systems integration from ICGS. Planned duration for the project is 30 years, with completion anticipated by 2027. As for the program budget, projected original cost awarded to systems integrator ICGS was $17 billion. However, the DHS revised and approved the baseline at $24.2 billion in November 2006. In addition, $6 billion was appropriated from fiscal year 2002 to 2009 for the project. The GAO recently found that the Deepwater Program has exceeded the 2007 cost and schedule baselines, and it is likely not on track to meet its asset-level performance baseline. The GAO believes that the total cost of Deepwater is currently at $28 billion, $3.8 billion over the 2007 baseline, and that several individual assets will not be completed by the 2027 timeline (Byrd, Cochran, Price, & Rogers, 2008).

Acquisition management represents significant challenges for DHS. All acquisition projects are behind schedule, over cost, and not meeting initial performance specifications. Along with Deepwater, two more DHS projects, Secure Border Initiative (SBI) and U.S. Visitor and Immigrant Status Indicator Technology, had issues with not meeting schedule, cost, and initial performance specifications. These lapses indicate that DHS and its component agencies lacked the project management competencies to optimally manage sophisticated acquisitions projects.

3.6.2 Consult the Business Community when Relevant

Consulting the relevant business community ensures that the appropriate business processes are aligned as well as the delivery of value for money. The Libra Project includes renovation and upgrade of IT Systems for UK magistrates' courts. Magistrates' courts committees use different systems and have different working practices. Current systems have been inadequate for many years and do not allow information to be shared electronically with other courts. Electronic information transfer to other enforcement agencies is piecemeal. The government decided in the early 1990s to develop a national standard IT strategy for magistrates' courts. The Libra Project was initiated in October 1996 with an original planned contract duration of 10.5 years. However, due to multiple delays, the project was completed with multiple extensions after 14.5 years in 2011. The original project budget was £184 million over 10.5 years, whereas the actual revised contract was for £319 million over 14.5 years.

The roll out of Libra was planned in two phases. The first phase provided new case facilities, including links into agencies such as police, television licensing, and the Driver and Vehicle Licensing Agency, and for management and enforcement of fines. The second phase enhanced the fine account administration and included facilities to accept on-line payments, track pre-court means information, and enforce the sanctions provided for by the Courts Act. The project finished within its original scope but with delays and added cost. The delays caused problems with the implementation of the Courts Act requiring resource-intensive manual workarounds, as the legacy IT systems could not support the sanctions, which were designed to be implemented using Libra phase 2.

Selection of a private sector company for a government project created some communication issues. The project was awarded to International Computers Limited (ICL), the sole bidder on the project. ICL was a large British computer hardware and software company, which operated from 1968 until 2002 when ICL migrated its brand and was renamed after its parent company to Fujitsu Services. Since this project was contracted to an outside company which did not communicate well with the customer, there were many consultation issues, and information sharing became problematic. In addition, there was pressure from the customer's organization to complete the project in order to increase efficiency and cut spending. Meetings were held with the company to renegotiate contracts for more reasonable expectations, resulting in additional contracts with the contractor. Moreover, meeting the system requirements was a major issue within the project environment, system design took longer than expected, and system integration was difficult, due to the massive size of the project.

As for recommendations, IT system changes should support redesigned business processes. Undertaking one without the other is unlikely to deliver value for money. Standardizing IT systems across a number of disparate bodies is only likely to be effective if the appropriate business processes of those bodies are also aligned. To encourage suitable bids for a particular contract, departments should survey the market and consult the business community to establish the level of interest in the project and to assess whether their proposals are likely to be attractive to potential bidders. Departments should take it as a warning sign that their proposed projects may not be workable if few bidders show initial interest and others withdraw as the procurement process continues. When a department unavoidably finds itself in a single tender situation, it should take special care to ensure that value for money is not at risk. Precautionary measures might, for example, include developing a "should cost" model to assess the reasonableness of a bid.

3.6.3 Coordinate the Project with Existing Operations

Coordinating government projects with existing operations is vital for success. Owners and project managers often need to work with existing facilities to build new projects or should consider joining new and existing projects once new projects are complete. It could be problematic if those issues are not planned ahead or addressed adequately.

METRO Rail is the 7.5-mile (12.1 km) light rail line in Houston, TX (USA). Commencement of construction on the new North, Southeast, and East End lines was tentatively scheduled to be completed no sooner than 2014, according to an announcement by METRO in September 2010. In August 2010, METRO reported a budget shortfall of $49 million, which has halted progress on the University/Blue Line. The line has already received a final Federal Record of Decision but METRO has made no official announcement regarding when construction will start or how the line will be funded. METRO previously claimed that the completion of construction and opening of the Red Line Extension would be by 2013 and the East End/Green Line by 2014. However, between the need to rebid the rail car construction contract, the potential loss of the $40 million invested in Construcciones y Auxiliar de Ferrocarriles due to the rebid, the budget shortfall, and the delays now inherent in construction due to the uncertainty of gaining the $900 million from the Federal Transit Administration, METRO announced on September 9, 2010, that the commencement dates for the North, Southeast, and East End lines were pushed back to 2014. Original plans anticipated project completion within 60 months and $300 million; however, current estimates are that the project will be completed in 96 months from commencement date, with 3 years delay.

The Houston METRO Rail project demonstrates the vital importance of project coordination with existing operations for successful government projects. Contractors were required to work on existing facilities to build the project, which turned out to be problematic. Once complete, the Southeast and East End Lines will join the existing Main Street Line to connect residents and visitors from far and wide to business, education, and government centers, along with sporting events, cultural and entertainment venues, hotels, restaurants, and more in the heart of the city. Parsons is responsible for designing, building, operating, and maintaining the expanded light rail system, which will include four new corridors, totaling approximately 20 miles of light rail transit, 32 stations, storage and inspection facilities, and a major renovation to the existing operations center. METRO Rail shared Metro's existing communications infrastructure, under a turnkey contract administered by Siemens, including catenary, sub-stations, signaling, fare collection, communications, and central control. However, working on the existing facilities for the new project was not an easy task. Increasing transit system capacity (where feasible and affordable) and improving operations management of existing facilities requires a high level of planning, alignment, management, and implementation among stakeholders in order to make the project successful.

3.6.4 Establish Interagency Agreements for Cross-Agency Projects

It is recommended that future interagency agreements establish clear and well-defined roles and responsibilities for all parties participating in the contract administration process, including those involved in the invoice review process, such as contracting officers, technical points of contact, contracting officer's technical representatives, and contractor personnel with oversight and administrative roles.

FBI Trilogy was an IT project to introduce new systems infrastructure and upgrade existing investigative and intelligence applications, including establishing an enterprise network to enable communications among hundreds of domestic and foreign FBI locations. Trilogy consisted of three parts: (1) the Information Presentation Component (IPC) to upgrade the FBI's computer hardware and software; (2) the Transportation Network Component (TNC) to upgrade the FBI's communication network; and (3) the User Application Component (UAC) to upgrade and consolidate the FBI's five most important investigative applications (National Research Council, 2004). Because the Trilogy project was so large, the Department of Justice required the FBI to use two contractors for the three Trilogy components. The FBI combined the IPC and TNC portions of Trilogy into one enhancement, awarded it in 2001, and planned completion of this package in 37 months. The first two components were finished ahead of schedule in 35 months, and while IPC and TNC experienced cost overruns and schedule delays, both are currently still operating. The second contract for UAC was also awarded in 2001 and estimated project duration was 36 months. However, the FBI terminated the project after Trilogy's overall costs grew from $380 million to $537 million, the program fell behind schedule, and pilot testing showed that completion of Virtual Case File (VCF) under UAC was unfeasible and cost prohibitive.

Reasons cited for VCF's failure included poorly defined system requirements, ineffective requirements change control, limited contractor oversight, and human capital shortfalls due to no continuity in certain management positions and a lack of trained staff for key program positions. After more than four years of hard work and \$500 million, Trilogy has had little impact on the FBI's antiquated case-management system, which today remains a morass of mainframe green screens and vast stores of paper records. Also, 9/11 attacks piled enormous pressure onto the Trilogy project and altered the course of VCF dramatically. In light of our study, clearly defining the roles and responsibilities of each party in interagency agreements, particularly those related to reviewing and approving invoices, is a key factor for project success.

Chapter 4

Discussion

Government projects and programs are unique and complex, and hence suffer from a high rate of failure. In order to better understand the major reasons for failure and propose recommendations to enhance performance, this study has analyzed audit reports of 39 government projects and programs in three developed countries (United States, United Kingdom, and Australia). Data were collected from audit reports from the U.S. GAO, UK National Audit Office (NAO), and Australian National Audit Office (ANAO). This section elaborates the discussions based on the content analysis and statistical analysis of the data.

4.1 Most Common Frameworks and/or Principles Used

Across 39 projects and programs that were analyzed, the most commonly used framework and/or principles for successful projects were: research/forecasting (cost-benefit analysis, implementation studies, etc.), resource management, monitoring and evaluation (committees/ support groups), and a continuous or final review process. Key findings at the end of multiple project evaluations stated that these characteristics were directly responsible, in part, for the completion of projects in a satisfactory manner. Conversely, projects that failed had many layers of governance (complication and communication issues), did not have scheduled check-ins, and lacked cooperative efforts between units. Not all cases resulted in project terminations, but most required significant restructuring, including reduced scope, increased budgets, or extended time.

4.2 Critical Factors Affecting Project Performance

Based on our data, we identified common factors affecting performance. We categorized these factors into those affecting poor performance and those affecting good performance. Common factors for poor performance include:

- Lack of support from users;
- Underestimation of project complexity and cost; and
- Lack of leadership/management skills needed.

The most frequently cited issues were related to lack of project management skill and underestimation of project complexity/cost due to underperformed feasibility studies. Additionally inefficient allocation of resources, competing management styles, and other factors contributed to poor performance. Common factors affecting good performance include:

- Established timelines and check-points;
- Clear leadership and accountability;
- Quality planning; and
- Effective and comprehensive feasibility studies.

Additionally, projects that drew knowledge from multiple expert sources often resulted in faster completion times or decreased complications. Project groups that engaged multiple parties but maintained a clearly defined leader were able to utilize skilled individuals and avoid conflicts. One major risk in this tactic is the potential for lack of due diligence. If this occurs when seeking a potential contractor, references may not be contacted or examined, providing an opportunity for an underperforming player to join the group. This is easily mitigated by proper due diligence in pre-screening efforts, but has been skipped in some instances to reduce planning timelines and cost.

4.3 Statistical Analysis

To better understand the importance of project management in the government sector, all collected projects have been evaluated on a seven-point Likert scale for the following measures:

- Project management capabilities—represented by the government department's use and implementation of project management methodologies, tools, and techniques.
- Project management success—represented by the project manager's performance in achieving the project plan in terms of schedule, cost, and scope/quality.
- Project ownership success—represented by the project owner's performance in realizing the business case (Zwikael & Smyrk, 2012).

Statistical analyses suggest positive and significant correlations among the three measures. These results mean that project management is positively related to project performance of both project management and project ownership success. The correlation table is presented in Table 1.

Following the positive results from the correlation analysis, we tested whether project management capabilities have a positive impact on project management success using a more robust regression analysis. Results were controlled for project duration and cost, as these are variables that can potentially explain the variance in the dependent variable. Results are presented in Table 2.

Results show that neither of the control variables have significant impact on project management success. The only variable

Table 1. Correlation analysis

		Project management capabilities	Project management success	Project ownership success
Project management capabilities	Correlation		**0.505****	**0.512****
	Significance (2-tailed)		0.002	0.002
	N		34	35
Project management success	Correlation			**0.534****
	Significance (2-tailed)			0.001
	N			35
Project ownership success	Correlation			
	Significance (2-tailed)			
	N			

**Correlation is significant at the 0.01 level (2-tailed).

that significantly impacts the dependent variable is "project management capabilities" (Standardized Coefficient = 0.539, significance value = 0.002). The regression results are significant (F = 5.329**) with 35.5% of the variance explained by these variables. The conclusion from this analysis is that project management positively and significantly improves project management success.

Table 2. Regression analysis

	Standardized coefficient	t value	Significance value
Project management capabilities	0.539	3.456	**0.002****
Project duration	-0.267	-1.495	0.146
Project cost	-0.150	-0.866	0.394

*$p<0.05$; **$p<0.01$; ***$p<0.001$

Further, the impact of project management capabilities on project management success was tested for four project type dimensions (Shenhar & Dvir, 2007). All analyses were controlled for project duration and cost. Results suggest project management has the following impact:

- Novelty–project management positively affects performance in low and medium levels of novelty (derivative and platform), but not in breakthrough projects;
- Technology–project management positively affects performance in low to high levels of technology (low, medium, and high), but not in projects that involve super-high technology;
- Complexity–project management positively affects performance in very complex projects (array), but not in projects with low and medium levels of complexity (assembly, system); and
- Pace–project management positively affects performance in time-critical projects, but not in regular, fast, and blitz projects.

4.4 Project Typology

Project characteristics (novelty, degree of technical difficulty, system complexity, and pace) are not definitively linked to project success. Projects may be complex, high-tech systems, but still complete on time and according to last approved budgets. Instead, it is important to further examine the project management techniques that have contributed to successful or unsuccessful projects. Good performance can be attributed to project management efforts, particularly in the early stages of development. Projects with a greater amount of planning and forecasting appear to have received higher scores than other projects in terms of their overall success and stakeholder satisfaction. Meanwhile, poor performance has been attributed to too many "players," lack of organizational structure and timelines, and competing interests. These factors resulted in reduced scope, increased expenditure, or in some instances, cancellation of projects.

4.5 Additional Key Findings and Implications

Additional key findings from the content analysis are summarized in terms of status of projects completed, key reasons for performance outcome, and most commonly used project management principles, as shown in Table 3.

Table 3. Analysis of key findings of government projects and programs

Attributes/ points of interest	Strengths	Weaknesses	Others
Status of projects	• Some projects have been completed 100%, within original scope and budget. Data has shown that it is possible to complete projects earlier than planned and under budget.	• A majority of government projects fail to be completed within the original scope, budget, or timeline. This results in stakeholder displeasure, additional cost to taxpayers, and other consequences.	
Key reasons for performance outcome	• Good performance can be attributed to project management efforts, particularly in the early stages of development. Projects with a greater amount of planning and forecasting appear to be more successful in terms of their overall success and stakeholder satisfaction.	• Poor performance has been attributed to, e.g., too many "players," lack of organizational structure and timelines, and competing interests. These factors resulted in reduced scope, increased expenditure, or in some instances, cancellation of projects.	• Project characteristics (novelty, degree of technical difficulty, system complexity, and pace) are not definitively linked to project success. Projects may be complex, high-tech systems, but still are capable of being completed on time and according to last approved budgets.
Most common project management principles	• Research/forecasting (cost-benefit analysis, implementation studies, etc.) • Resource management • Monitoring and evaluation (committees/support groups) • Review processes	• Many layers of governance (complication and communication issues) • Lack of scheduled check-ins • Failure to act cooperatively between units	

Chapter 5

Concluding Remarks

Previous literature suggests government projects tend to have long duration, large budgets, multiple stakeholders, and a great deal of uncertainty. This study has identified additional key characteristics of government projects and programs, which are:

- Non-financial benefits;
- Susceptibility to political environment and dynamics;
- Mandated project management process;
- Large and complex megaprojects;
- Long product life cycle; and
- Multiple stakeholders.

Stakeholders should examine the aforementioned positive and negative aspects of government projects in order to understand potential pitfalls and advantages of pursuing particular paths. This is especially important for time-sensitive projects, because improper choices can result in delays. The research team has analyzed the audit reports of 39 projects and programs. Twenty-eight key recommendations from this study are summarized in Table 4.

These recommendations are discussed and illustrated in our study. Their implementations can support policy makers, government officials, project managers, and the general public. This research supports the importance of adopting project management principles, tools, and techniques for governmental

Table 4. Six key characteristics and 28 recommendations for government projects and programs

Key characteristics	Recommendations
Non-financial benefits	1. Identify clear non-financial benefits in the business case
	2. Ensure that target benefits are realistic and achievable
	3. Establish an agreed-upon evaluation methodology for project benefits
	4. Evaluate the impact of the project on the achievement of strategic goals
Political environment	5. Consider legal consultation to ensure that proposed ideas are in line with current legislation
	6. Consider financial consultation to improve understanding of economic aspects of the project
	7. Ensure that the project is aligned with agencies' strategies
	8. Consider public-private partnership (PPP) when appropriate
	9. Ensure PPPs are economically feasible
	10. Provide project managers more authority
Formal process	11. Establish and follow government project management framework and processes
	12. Follow formal planning and estimating processes that incorporate lessons learned
	13. Follow a formal risk management process
	14. Follow formal project monitoring and change management processes
	15. Establish and follow project governance framework
Megaprojects	16. Develop a base cost estimate and Integrated Master Schedule for megaprojects
	17. Align the project cost with the yearly budget cycle
	18. Consider off-the-shelf solutions over high-risk new development when possible
	19. Split programs into smaller, more manageable projects for tight project control
	20. Develop a contingency plan and monitor risks
Long product life cycle	21. Identify training needs for long projects
	22. Ensure robust design and quality management process
	23. Reduce occasions of using unapproved (too advanced) technologies
Multiple stakeholders	24. Engage procurement personnel to the project team
	25. Consult the business community when relevant
	26. Coordinate the project with existing operations
	27. Establish interagency agreements for cross-agency projects
	28. Ensure effective collaboration with procurement personnel and an effective acquisition process

projects and programs that would result in enhanced performance. The project management community can use this study
to extend knowledge of government projects and programs. For
example, the next edition of the PMI's *Government Extension
to the PMBOK® Guide Third Edition* can integrate some of the
recommendations included in this study.

We would like to recommend project audit reports as a useful
source of information for teams implementing new endeavors.
By examining past errors, it is possible to encounter or develop
ways to make a process more efficient. In other words, although
some physical aspects of projects may be more easily controlled
(cost of goods) and result in time decreases, systems are much
more difficult to quickly establish.

Additionally, without proper systems in place to facilitate
the progression of these inputs to the final product, accelera-
tion of the over-all project timeline becomes impossible. For
example, an Australian audit report of the FiReControl Project
revealed elements that led to that project's complete failure. The
project's mission was to improve the resilience, efficiency, and
technology of the Fire and Rescue Service by replacing 46 local
control rooms with a network of nine purpose-built regional
control centers using a national computer system to handle
calls, mobilize equipment, and manage incidents. Although it
was terminated without being completed, the project team was
able to develop a comprehensive list of suggestions for future
management personnel that apply to all government efforts:

- Hold contracts to account;
- Work to align project and purpose;
- Develop appropriate management capacity;
- Understand and resolve cultural and technical obstacles;
- Ensure users are fully invested in the project;
- Ensure reports/proposals are not overly biased;

- Ensure that expected costs/benefits and timetables are realistic;
- Establish a critical path; and
- Develop transparent control procedures.

This comprehensive list not only summarizes key points made by other auditing groups, but also solidifies and simplifies them. By following the nine points mentioned above, project managers will experience increased success rates. By continuing to explore various project management issues and publish the findings through audit reports, governments will be able to learn from past successes and failures and adapt the best practices for future projects and programs.

Appendix

Appendix A—List of 39 projects and programs that have been analyzed in this study

#	Project name	Country	Sector	Government owner
1	Secure Border Initiative Network Project	US	Mixed (IT, communications, construction, etc.)	Department of Homeland Security (DHS)
2	2010 Census (23rd national decennial census)	US	Federal Government	Bureau of the Census (Department of Commerce and Labor)
3	The Coast Guard's Project Deepwater	US	Defense	Coast Guard
4	Australian Broadband Guarantee	Australia	Public	Australian Government, Department of Broadband, Communications and the Digital Economy
5	DOD Base Realignment and Closure	US	Public–Federal Government	Secretary of Defense/ U.S. President
6	Benefit Card Payment	UK	Public	Department of Social Security, Post Office Counters Ltd.
7	Boom Gates for Railway Crossings	Australia	Infrastructure	Department of Infrastructure and Transport
8	C-17 Globemaster III Heavy Airlifter	Australia	Aircraft (defense)	Royal Australian Air Force
9	CrimTrac	Australia	Law Enforcement Information Systems	Australian Attorney General
10	East Kimberly Development	Australia	Infrastructure	Office of Northern Australia
11	FiReControl	UK	Technology	Department for Communities and Local Government
12	Future Combat Systems	US	Department of Defense	Defense Advanced Research Projects Agency, Army
13	Joint Strike Fighter	US	Military Aircraft (Sullivan 2)	Department of Defense (Sullivan 2)
14	LIBRA	UK	IT Systems	Magistrates' Courts Committees
15	Mandurah Entrance Road	Australia	Infrastructure	Department of Infrastructure and Transport
16	Multi-role Helicopter	Australia	Military	Royal Australian Navy and Army
17	The National Programme for Information Technology in National Health Care Service	UK	National Health Care	Department of Health
18	National Security Hotline	Australia	National Security	Emergency Management Australia Attorney-General Department
19	Modernization & Associated Restructuring Program	US	Federal Government	National Weather Service

#	Project name	Country	Sector	Government owner
20	The Channel Deepening Project	Australia	Infrastructure	Department of Transport and the Department of Sustainability and Environment
21	V-22 OSPREY Joint Vertical Lift Aircraft Program	US	V/STOL transport	U.S. Marine Corps U.S. Air Force U.S. Army – abandoned project May 1983
22	Yucca Mountain	US	Federal Government	Department of Energy, Nuclear Regulatory Commission
23	Springfield Interchange Project (Known as the "Mixing Bowl")	US	Transportation	Federal Highway Administration provided 90% funding. Virginia Department of Transportation
24	San Francisco – Oakland Bay Bridge Retrofit/Replacement Project of East Span	US	Transportation	Federal Highway Administration and the California Department of Transportation
25	Dallas Area Rapid Transit ORANGE LINE TO NORTH IRVING/DFW	US	Transportation	Federal Transit Administration/Shaw Stone and Webster
26	Los Angeles Metro – Expo Phase 1	US	Transportation	Exposition Construction Authority (Expo), Funding by Metro
27	Houston METRO Rail	US	Transportation	Federal Transit Administration Operator: Metropolitan Transit Authority of Harris County (METRO)
28	London Heathrow Airport – Terminal 5	UK	Transportation – Aviation	British Airports Authority Limited Operator: Heathrow Airport Limited
29	The Channel Tunnel	UK	Transportation - Railways	Eurotunnel
30	Australian Defence Force Project AIR 5077 Phase 3 (Project Wedgetail) Airborne Early Warning and Control Program	Australia	Defence/Security	Defence Materiel Organisation Department of Defence
31	Homeowner Insulation Program	Australia	Infrastructure	The Department of Climate Change and Energy Efficiency, formerly the Department of the Environment, Water, Heritage and the Arts and Medicare
32	Centrelink IT Refresh Program	Australia	Information Technology	Centrelink
33	Project AIR87: Armed Reconnaissance Helicopter (ARH Tiger)	Australia	Defence and Security	Department of Defence, Defence Materiel Organisation
34	M7 Motorway, New South Wales, Australia	Australia	Infrastructure	Roads and Traffic Authority New South Wales Government, with funding from the Federal Government
35	Digital Education Revolution: National Secondary Schools Computer Fund project	Australia	IT/Education	Department of Education, Employment and Workplace Relations
36	Defense Integrated Military Human Resources System	US	IT/IS	U.S. Department of Defense
37	Trilogy	US	IT/IS	FBI
38	Sentinel	US	IT/IS	FBI
39	Navy Marine Corps Intranet program	US	IT/IS	U.S. Navy, Department of Defense

References

Australian National Audit Office. (2006). *Management of the personnel management key solution (PMKeyS) implementation project.* The Auditor General Audit Report. Commonwealth of Australia.

Australian National Audit Office. (2007). *Customs' cargo management re-engineering project.* The Auditor General Audit Report. Commonwealth of Australia.

Arditi, D., Akan, G. T., & Gurdamar, S. (1985). Reasons for delays in public projects in Turkey. *Construction Management and Economics, 3*(2), 171–181.

Assaf, S. A., Al-Khalil, M., & Al-Hazmi, M. (1995). Causes of delay in large building construction projects. *Journal of Management in Engineering.* ASCE, *11*, 45–50

Baldry, D. (1998). The evaluation of risk management in public sector capital projects. *International Journal of Project Management, 16*(1), 35–41.

Barclay, C. (2008). Towards an integrated measurement of IS project performance: The project performance scorecard. *Information Systems Frontiers, 10*(3), 331–345.

Bhuiyan, N., & Thomson, V. (1999). The use of continuous approval methods in defense acquisition projects. *International Journal of Project Management, 17*(2), 121–129.

Boyd, D., & Chinyio, D. (2006). Understanding the construction client. Oxford, England: Blackwell.

Bruelious, N., Flyvbjerg, B., & Rothengatter, W. (1998). Big decision, big risks: Improving accountability in megaprojects. *International Review of Administrative Science, 64*, 423–440.

Bueno, J. C. (2010). Who's afraid of political risks? Retrieved from http://kluwerconstructionblog.com/2010/08/12/whos -afraid-of-political-risks/

Byrd, R. C., Cochran, T., Price, D. E., & Rogers, H. (2008). Coast Guard—Change in Course Improves Deepwater Management and Oversight, but Outcome Still Uncertain. Retrieved from http://www.gao.gov/new.items/d08745.pdf

Capka, J. R. (2004). Megaprojects—They are a different breed. *Public Roads*, *68*(1). Retrieved from http://www.fhwa.dot .gov/publications/publicroads/04jul/01.cfm

Chan, D. W. M., & Kumaraswamy, M. M. (1995). A study of the factors affecting construction durations in Hong Kong. *Construction Management and Economics*, *13*(4), 319–333.

Conahan, F. C. National Security and International Affairs Division. (1986). Report to Congressional Requesters: DOD Acquisition - Case Study of the Navy V-22 Osprey Joint Vertical Lift Aircraft Program. Retrieved from United States General Accounting Office website: http://archive .gao.gov/d4t4/130575.pdf

DPAC (Department of Premier and Cabinet). (2011). Tasmanian government project management guidelines. Retrieved from http://www.egovernment.tas.gov.au/__data/assets/pdf_ file/0019/147511/Tasmanian_Government_Project_Man- agement_Guidelines_V7_0_July_2011_2.pdf

Dvir, D. (2005). Transferring projects to their final users: The effect of planning and preparations for commissioning on project success. *International Journal of Project Management*, *23*, 257–265.

Dvir, D., & Lechler, T. (2004). Plans are nothing changing plans is everything: The impact of changes on project success. *Research Policy*, *33*(1), 1–15.

Dvir, D., Raz, T., & Shenhar, A. J. (2003). An empirical analysis of the relationships between project planning and project success. *International Journal of Project Management*, *21*, 89–95.

Egeland, B. (2009). Project planning: Evaluating the political environment. Retrieved from http://pmtips.net/project-planning-evaluating-political-environment/

Flyvbjerg, B., Holm, M. K. S., & Buhl, S. (2003a). How common and how large are cost overruns in transport infrastructure project? *Transport Reviews. 23*(1), 71–88.

Flyvbjerg, B., Bruzelious, N., & Rothengatter W. (2003b). *Megaproject and risk: An anatomy of ambition.* Cambridge: Cambridge University Press.

Flyvbjerg, B., Holm, M. K. S., & Buhl, S. (2004). What causes cost overrun in transport infrastructure projects? *Transport Reviews. 24*(1), 3–18.

Flyvbjerg, B. (2007). Cost overrun and demand shortfalls in urban rail and other infrastructure, *Transportation Planning and Technology. 30*(1), 9–30.

Frimpong, Y., & Oluwoye, J. (2003). Significant factors causing delay and cost overruns in construction of groundwater projects in Ghana. *Journal of Construction Research, 4*(2), 175–187.

Gil, N. (2007, August). *The management of large engineering (physical infrastructure) projects: Debating a research agenda.* Presentation material at the 2007 Professional Development Workshop, Academy of Management Conference, Philadelphia, PA.

GAO. (1986). *DOD acquisition: Strengthening capabilities of key personnel in systems acquisition.* Washington, DC: Government Accounting Office.

GAO. (2002). *Military transformation: Army actions needed to enhance formation of future interim brigade combat team.* Washington, DC: Government Accountability Office.

GAO. (2004a). *Defense acquisitions: The army's future combat systems' features, risks, and alternatives.* Washington, DC: Government Accountability Office.

GAO. (2004b). *Department of defense: Long-standing problems continue to impede financial and business management transformation*. Washington, DC: Government Accountability Office.

GAO. (2005a). *Defense acquisitions: Future combat systems challenges and prospects for success*. Washington, DC: Government Accountability Office.

GAO. (2005b). *DOD business systems modernization: Navy ERP adherence to best business practices critical to avoid past failures*. Washington, DC: Government Accountability Office.

GAO. (2006). *Defense acquisitions: Improved business case is needed for FCS's successful outcome*. Washington, DC: Government Accountability Office.

GAO. (2007a). *Defense acquisitions: Future combat system risks underscore the importance of oversight*. Washington, DC: Government Accountability Office.

GAO. (2007b). *Joint strike fighter: Progress made and challenges remain*. Washington, DC: Government Accountability Office.

GAO. (2007c). *Cost estimating guide: Best practices for estimating and managing program costs, exposure draft*. Washington, DC: Government Accountability Office.

GAO. (2007d). *Defense acquisitions: Assessments of selected weapons programs*. Washington, DC: Government Accountability Office.

GAO. (2010). *Secure border initiative: DHS needs to strengthen management and oversight of its prime contractor*. Washington, DC: Government Accountability Office.

Han, S. H., Yun, S. M., Kim, H., Kwak, Y. H., Park, H. K., & Lee, S. H. (2009). Analyzing schedule delay of megaproject: Lessons learned from Korea Train eXpress (KTX). *IEEE Transactions on Engineering Management*. 56(2), 243–256.

Huemann, M., Keegan, A. E., & Turner, J.R. (2007). Human resource management in the project oriented organization – A review. *International Journal of Project Management*, 25(3), 315–323.

Jolivet, F., & Navarre, C. (1996). Large-scale projects, self-organizing and meta-rules: Towards new forms of management. *International Journal of Project Management, 14*(5), 265–271.

Kwak, Y.H., & Smith, B. (2009). Managing risks in mega defense acquisition projects: Performance, policy, and opportunities. *International Journal of Project Management, 27*(8), 812–820.

Kwak, Y.H., & Anbari, F.T. (2010). *Project management in government: An introduction to earned value management.* IBM Center for the Business of Government Report.

Kwak, Y.H., & Anbari, F.T. (2012). History, practices, and future of earned value management (EVM) in government: Perspectives from NASA. *Project Management Journal, 43*(1), 77–90.

Kwak, Y.H., Walewski, J., Sleeper, D., & Sadatsafavi, H. (2014). What Can We Learn from The Hoover Dam: that Influenced Modern Project Management. *International Journal of Project Managent, 32*(2), 256–264. doi:10.1016/j.ijproman.2013.04.002.

Lancaster, P. J. (2001). Not just bricks and mortar. In P. J. Lancaster with E. S. Plotkin & J. N. Lerner (Eds.), *Construction in cities: Social, environmental, political, and economic concerns.* Boca Raton, FL: CRC Press LLC.

Lyer, K. C., & Jha, K. N. (2006). Critical factors affecting schedule performance: Evidence from Indian construction projects. *Journal of Construction Engineering and Management*, ASCE, *132*(8), 871–881.

Lovallo, D., & Kahneman, D. (2003). Delusions of success. *Harvard Business Review, 81*(7), 56–63.

Majid, M. Z. & McCaffer, R. (1998). Factors of non-excusable delays that influence contractors' performance. *Journal of Management in Engineering*, ASCE *14*(3), 42–49.

Merrow, E. W., McDonnell, L. & Argüden, R. Y. (1988). *Understanding the outcomes of megaprojects: A quantitative analysis of very large civilian projects.* Santa Monica, CA: Rand Corporation.

Morris, P. W. G., & Hough, G.H. (1987). *The anatomy of major projects: A study of the reality of project management.* New York: Wiley, Chichester.

Mortimer Review. (2008). *Going to the next level: The report of the defence procurement and sustainment review, 2008.* Retrieved from http://www.defence.gov.au/publications /mortimerReview.pdf

NAO. (2000). *The cancellation of the benefits payment card project.* London: UK National Audit Office.

National Research Council. (2004). *A review of the FBI's trilogy information technology program.* Washington, DC: The National Research Council of the National Academies.

Office of Government Commerce (OGC). (2007). *Managing successful programmes.* Norwich, UK: The Stationery Office,.

Park, J. R., Park, Y. K., & Kim, S. B. (2005). *Lesson learned from national policy construction project.* CEO Information, Samsung Economic Research Institute, vol. 491.

Patanakul, P., & Omar, S. S. (2010, July). *Why mega IS/IT projects fail: Major problems and what we learned from them.* Proceeding of Portland International Conference on Management of Engineering and Technology (PICMET '10), Bangkok, Thailand.

Pinto, J. K. & Slevin, D. P. (1987). Critical factors in successful project implementation. *IEEE Transactions on Engineering Management, EM-34,* 22–27.

Project Management Institute. (2006). *Government extension to the PMBOK® guide third edition.* Newtown Square, PA: Author.

Shenhar, A.J. & Dvir, D. (1996). Toward a typological theory of project management. *Research Policy, 25,* 607–632.

Shenhar, A.J. (1998). From theory to practice: Toward a typology of project-management styles. *IEEE Transactions on Engineering Managenent, EM-45*(1), 33–48.

Shenhar, A.J. & Bonen, Z. (1997). The new taxonomy of systems: Toward an adaptive systems engineering framework. *IEEE Transactions on Systems, Man and Cybernetics, 27*(2), 137–145.

Shenhar, A.J. & Dvir, D. (2007). Reinventing project management: The diamond approach to successful growth and innovation. Boston: Harvard Business School Press.

Strain, J.D. & Preece, D.A. (1999). Project Management and the integration of human factors in military system procurement. *International Journal of Project Management,* 17(5), 283–292.

Stannard, C.J. (1990). Managing a megaproject–The channel tunnel. *Long Range Planning, 23*(5), 49–62.

Thompson, M. (2007, September). V-22 Osprey: A flying shame. *Time Magazine.* Retrieved from http://www.time.com/time/magazine/article/0,9171,1666282,00.html

Tysseland, B.E. (2008). Life cycle cost based procurement decisions: A case study of Norwegian defence procurement projects. *International Journal of Project Management, 26,* 366–375.

Williams, T. (2003). Assessing extension of time delays on major projects. *International Journal of Project Management, 21*(1), 19–26.

Williams, T. (1999). The need for new paradigms for complex projects. *International Journal of Project Management, 17*(5), 269–273.

Williams, T. (2004). Identifying the hard lessons from projects— easily. *International Journal of Project Management, 22*(5), 273–279.

Yeo, K.T. (1995). Planning and learning in major infrastructure development: Systems perspectives. *International Journal of Project Management, 13*(5), 287–293.

Zwikael, O., & Smyrk, J. R. (2011). *Project management for the creation of organizational value*. London, UK: Springer-Verlag.

Zwikael, O., & Smyrk, J. (2012). A general framework for gauging the performance of initiatives to enhance organizational value. *British Journal of Management, 23*, S6–S22.